CLB 1664
© 1986 Illustrations and text: Colour Library Books Ltd.,
    Guildford, Surrey, England.
Text filmsetting by Acesetters Ltd., Richmond, Surrey, England.
All rights reserved.
Printed and bound in Spain by Cronion, S.A.
1986 edition published by Crescent Books, distributed by Crown Publishers, Inc.
ISBN 0 517 61964 4
h g f e d c b a

LANDSCAPES OF THE
GRAND CANYON

CRESCENT BOOKS
NEW YORK

In 1976, 3.02 million people set an attendance record at Grand Canyon National Park and visitors have come close to breaking the record every year since.

But in 1857, when the Federal Government sent out an expedition to see what might be there, the official report said:

"Ours has been the first and will doubtless be the last party of whites to visit this profitless locality. It seems intended by nature that the Colorado River along the greater portion of its majestic way shall be forever unvisited and undisturbed."

The explorer was half right. Though the Grand Canyon hasn't been "undisturbed" for as many as 600 million years, the change that has taken place in the last 130 is all but imperceptible. And if the annual number of visitors hovers around the three million mark, it is still one of the few places on earth where total solitude is still possible in a setting that looked the same before humans existed.

The average Grand Canyon visitor spends three hours in the Park. According to some observers, many spend a half hour looking out over the rim and the rest of the time looking through the gift shop. Some are amazed that there is no elevator to take them down to the bottom or a bridge to get them across to the other side! Some, it is said, miss the Canyon completely. But how it is possible to miss a 300-mile long gash that's a mile deep and almost a dozen miles wide is hard to imagine. But if it's true, it's also very sad.

It is possible to walk a short distance from the village and find a spot where it seems no other human has ever been. And from that spot, looking ten miles across to the North Rim, it is easily possible to imagine that there are no other humans on earth. As you look at a seemingly endless configuration of terraces leading down to a bottom you know must be there, but can't see, and as you let the colors wash into your soul, you can't help wondering if, indeed, there is any other life on earth. Of course there is, and it is all around you. Swallows dart in and out of view, ravens soar over your head. Over in the brush a chipmunk pokes its head out for a look around and vanishes with the scolding of a squirrel who, you notice, may be the biggest squirrel you ever saw. Then a lizard darts up from below. You glance down to see where it came from and you notice a clump of wildflowers clinging to the edge of the rocks as though the view required just a little extra touch of color.

Far below, you may notice a little train of pack mules. If you can see them, they are probably about halfway down the Bright Angel Trail at a place known as Indian Gardens. The trail is one of nearly a dozen that lead down to the bottom of the Canyon and it is the one most frequently used by the 130 mules who, like so many other wonders in the Park, are in the employ of the Fred Harvey Amfac Resort Company.

Visitors who have had the foresight to make advance reservations find the mule ride an experience they never forget. Most have never ridden a mule before, of course, but it doesn't matter to the beast, who has seen it all before. Many have funny feelings about high places, too, and the animals seem to take some sort of perverse pleasure in exploiting the fear. Actually, the mules are pretty good survivors, but they like to eat as they go along and if a willow is close to the edge, well, who's afraid of a 500-foot drop?

Actually, though the mules don't seem too responsive to the sensibilities of the loads on their backs, they've been

Previous pages: sunset seen from Desert View Lookout. Facing page: a view from Mohave Point, West Rim Drive, South Rim.

down the trail hundreds of times and aren't in the habit of losing customers for Fred Harvey, much less putting their own lives in any danger.

The Bright Angel Trail is an earthquake fault that runs diagonal to the Canyon. It was improved over the centuries by animals and then by Indians who farmed the plateau called the Tonto Shelf halfway down. It was further improved in the 1890s by a pair of promoters who said they were going to set up a mine in the Canyon but wound up mining the pockets of other prospectors by charging tolls to use the trail. Over the years since it has been improved even more and includes emergency telephones and drinking fountains.

The Bright Angel and the Kaibab Trail meet just before the mule-riders reach the Colorado River. The river is crossed by a 420-foot suspension bridge that was built in 1928, the same year the all man-made Kaibab Trail was put into operation. The trip to that point takes four or five hours, just enough time for travelers to get stiff from sitting and to notice an odd feeling in their right hand, which has been pressed tight to the saddle pommel most of the way. They haven't seen much of the river on the way down, but at this point it is in constant view as the mules trudge along an almost level trail blasted into the side of the cliff. Once the bridge has been crossed, there is only another half mile to go to reach Phantom Ranch, where the smarter travelers have arranged to stay a few days. The Ranch is comfortable, not at all primitive as you might expect considering the location. The food is good and the water from Bright Angel Creek, which rushes down through a canyon to join the Colorado nearby, is icy cold and possibly the best drinking water on the face of the earth.

Of course, Phantom Ranch is only a destination. It's the trip itself that counts. For the first 500 feet or so, the stone along the trail is not much different from the surface. It is called Kaibab limestone, believed to have been the sediment at the bottom of a sea that covered this part of the Southwest about 300 million years ago. Actually, the top layer of gray limestone was apparently caused by two different oceans. The space between them is marked by a small horizontal band of red stone.

That 500 feet represents a leap back to the Paleozoic Era, which predates the appearance of reptiles and of mammals. The next era represented on the way down is the Permian, represented in the cliff walls by yellow sandstone. This 400-foot layer is marked by more undulating lines, which were caused by the shifting sands of a prehistoric desert. It took some 30 million years to create the yellow section which rests on top of another layer of limestone that is called the "Red Wall." It is 550 feet deep, believed to have been created by the sediment from a great ocean that covered most of western North America for some 70 million years. Though the band that runs along each of the Canyon's walls is a brilliant red color, the color is just on the surface, the stone having been stained by iron deposits.

The base of the Red Wall is the Tonto Platform, 3200 feet down from the rim. It represents a sort of oasis among the rocks of the Canyon. Trees and plants grow, if not thrive, here and a large spring provides water for the settlement up on the rim.

In moving between the Red Wall and the Tonto Platform, two eras of geological time have been lost, probably to erosion, but the history of the earth picks up again as if nothing happened. The trail winds down into the remains of the Cambrian period, the era when one-celled animals began swimming in the seas. As the mule plods along, the rocks it kicks up are noticeably different down here than at any other point along the trail. They're much darker in color and the markings are different. Geologists call them Algonkian rocks, and some of them are said to date back to the Proterozoic Era, which began more than 2500 million years ago. They are super-hard rocks with glittering traces of quartz in them, and were probably once the stuff of huge mountains that rose and fell long before life was even but a dream.

But below that layer is yet another. The oldest exposed rocks on the face of the earth are down here at the bottom of the Grand Canyon. They date back something in the neighborhood of 4600 million years ago, to the Archean Era.

It's enough to boggle the mind. And the river is still cutting deeper. It carries an average of a half-million tons of sand and rocks through the Canyon each and every day. The bottom of the Grand Canyon is 2000 feet above sea level, which means that it can and will carve the Canyon that much deeper. At that point, the force of gravity will turn the mighty Colorado into a meandering brook. But don't hold your breath. It took more than 400 million years to cut through the first 2000 feet and many of the layers up there were a good bit softer. Your great grandchildren won't see anything different about the Grand Canyon than you'll see today.

What you see when you arrive at Phantom Ranch is a setting that could be a thousand other places in the west. There are trees and flowers, and birds flying overhead. And the buttes and cliffs hide the Canyon walls except in a few places. It isn't until you think that your car is a mile away, straight up, that you remember where you are.

And where you are is a place of splendid isolation. It is a place to explore, to stroll down to the river and marvel at its force, to stick a toe into the icy, incredibly clean water of Bright Angel Creek. There are side canyons that provide incredible vistas, and the 50-foot Ribbon Falls, a five-mile hike from the Ranch, where ferns have taken up residence in a spray-filled glen that makes you think of nothing quite as much as the Garden of Eden.

It's a place no one ever likes to leave. But when the time comes, the way up is usually via the Kaibab Trail, which is shorter, though steeper, than the Bright Angel Trail. That makes the trip easier on the visitors, but makes the mules a little grumpy.

Even people who have problems with high places and often make the trip with one hand over their eyes, peeking out every once in a while through spread fingers, say it is a trip worth taking. It can be tiring to people used to a sedentary life, but the reward is exhilaration. And a lifetime of memories.

The less intrepid, and those who didn't plan ahead, usually confine their Grand Canyon experience to exploring the South Rim and watching the light play wonderful tricks with the colors of the rocks. They look down and wonder, of course, but just as often they look across and wonder what's over there on the North Rim and why is all the activity here on this side?

The man they say started it all was John Hance, who arrived in the early 1880s and set up a mining camp. Like so many miners who tried to take riches from the Canyon, he discovered that it was too hard to get minerals up over the rim. But he liked the place and stayed and became the first to welcome visitors who came by stagecoach from Flagstaff. His camp, about 20 miles from the present Grand Canyon Village, was the official destination at the end of the two-day stagecoach ride. It wasn't long before he had a competitor in the form of Pete Berry, who built a hotel at Grand View Point in 1892 to supplement his income from a copper mine. Berry eventually sold out to William Randolph Hearst, who was on his way to making the Canyon his private preserve when the Santa Fe Railroad took over a line that had been built to serve the copper mines and connected it with their own main line. In 1904 the Fred Harvey Company built the El Tovar Hotel, and from then on there was no contest.

If there ever had been, the Canyon became a National Park in 1919, making all other claims moot. The Santa Fe was happy. Until service stopped in 1968, Grand Canyon was the only National Park served directly by a railroad.

But there is no bridge to the North Rim, of course, and the trip by automobile, though beautiful, is a long one. It is necessary to drive 215 miles to get to that spot ten miles away. The trip needs to be taken between June and October, too. The rest of the year the North Rim is snowbound.

It is generally agreed that the view of the Canyon from

the South Rim is the more dramatic, but they are so totally different from each other that there is no point debating which experience is more moving. The North Rim is about a thousand feet higher and so supports a vastly different assortment of plants and animals. The view from the edge is to the west, so it is better seen at sunrise than at sunset. But because it is so much higher, your eye takes you out across the South Rim to the countryside beyond, which isn't quite as beautiful as the countryside behind you.

It is a landscape dominated by Douglas firs, blue spruce and mahogany trees, and accented by delicate aspens. It is also broken up by side canyons that are as dramatic as the Grand Canyon itself, except for their size.

There is a hotel on the North Rim, almost directly across from Grand Canyon Village. Getting to it is as different an experience as the difference between the two sites. The last 20 miles of the trip are through a thick forest of evergreens with only an occasional glimpse at flower-strewn alpine meadows. There are flowers in the forest, too. Long-stemmed lupine grows everywhere, giving touches of yellow and blue to showy pink penstemon and fresh white daisies. Having come from the near-desert conditions of the South Rim, you're liable to forget where you are, but suddenly, just as is the case on the other side, the Canyon appears as if from nowhere, and somewhere back in the depths of your mind you hear some great dramatic chord of music.

Between the rim and the river below is a series of buttes that were named, along with so many other features on the Colorado River, by John Wesley Powell, who led the first expedition down the river in 1869. The buttes seem to have reminded him of the man-made landmarks in India and Siam. Shiva Temple is one of the biggest peaks in the group, rising some 4000 feet from the floor of the Canyon, and its neighbors have such exotic names as Zoroaster Temple and Brahma Temple. But one of them has the all-American name of Uncle Jimmy.

It was named for James Owens, a local character who made his living leading cougar-hunting safaris through the Kaibab Plateau. His most celebrated client was Theodore Roosevelt, who went hunting here in 1913 and, as happens to just about everybody, fell in love with the place.

Roosevelt said that the Grand Canyon was the one place in America that every American ought to see.

But it is much more than something to be seen. It is an experience, almost a religious one to many, that touches you in a very unusual way. Photographers have tried to capture it, painters have tried to duplicate it, writers have tried to describe it. But no one has ever been completely successful in communicating what the Grand Canyon does to you.

One of the earliest guide books published after the National Park was established probably said it best. The only way to describe the Grand Canyon, it said, is in the two words almost everyone utters when they see it for the first time:

"My God!"

Facing page: Mohave Point, along West Rim Drive on the South Rim of the Grand Canyon.

Previous pages: a hard
light enhances the natural
beauty of the Grand Canyon.
Above: a view from Hopi
Point of the vast gorge,
its mysteries hinted at as
it lies in shadows cast by
the low sun. Right: a
shadowed view from Mohave
Point. Facing page: (top)
the Canyon seen from Yaki
Point, its peaks tinted
golden by the late rays of
the afternoon sun. Bottom:
Duck on a Rock Viewpoint
and the Inner Gorge bathed
in sunshine.

The Grand Canyon, part of the Colorado Plateau, is made up of a complex system of gorges, ravines and canyons intersected by the Colorado River, and became a National Park in 1919. Previous pages: the Canyon seen from Yaki Point, on the South Rim. Above: the rock strata of the Canyon seen from Lipau Point and (left) visitors gazing across the Canyon from West Rim Drive. Facing page: (top) seen from the Watchtower, the Colorado River winds its way through the Canyon. Bottom: the Canyon in somber light beyond Mohave Point Lookout.

Previous pages: the peaks and buttes of the Grand Canyon seen from Navajo Point. This page and facing page top: mules and backpackers on the Bright Angel Trail. Muleback trips are a popular way of experiencing the splendor of the Canyon. Facing page: (bottom) layered cliffs viewed from West Rim Drive.

Previous pages: visitors view the awesome expanses of the Canyon from Navajo Point; a glimpse of the Colorado River is visible on the floor of the canyon. Above and right: peaks and canyons stretch out before the eye from Mather Point Lookout, their layered rock strata displaying many varying colors, from buff, grey and the most delicate greens through to orange and pink. Facing page: (top) the Colorado River winding its way along the Canyon floor west of Crystal Rapids, and (bottom) the eroded cliffs of Bright Angel Trail.

Previous pages: sunlit peaks and partly-shadowed gorges, (these pages) Bright Angel Trail, and (overleaf) the Canyon seen from Desert View.

Previous pages and left: wide views from Yaki Point. Above: sharp contrasts below Mohave Point, where the Canyon's asymmetry is typically pronounced. The reason for this asymmetry lies in a geological event that occurred millions of years ago. The rocks in this area were folded and uplifted to form the Kaibab Plateau. However, the uplift was slightly uneven, and the North Rim was raised almost a thousand feet higher than the South Rim. Facing page: (top) the river near Point Sublime, and (bottom) Wotans Throne from Yaki Point. Overleaf: Bright Angel Trail seen from El Tovar.

Previous pages: the swiftly-flowing Colorado River below Moran Point, named after Thomas Moran, the 19th-century landscape painter whose style was greatly influenced after he experienced the changing light-effects on the Grand Canyon. Above, left and facing page top: Bright Angel Trail viewed from West Rim Drive. The trail lies along an earthquake fault and was originally an animal track which became known to local Indians and which, in 1890, was opened up by two prospectors. Facing page: (bottom) red cliffs seen from Mohave Point, and (overleaf) from Moran Point.

Four-and-a-half miles down Bright Angel Trail (these pages) lie the Indian Gardens, an area once cultivated by the Havasupai Indians. From here, a branch trail leads across the Tonto Platform to Plateau Point, and the Bright Angel Trail continues to the Kaibab Suspension Bridge and Phantom Ranch. Facing page: (top) saddling up the mules at the start of Bright Angel Trail. Overleaf: a spectacular view from West Rim Drive.

It takes about three hours by mule to descend the Bright Angel Trail (previous pages, these pages and overleaf) as far as the platform, and another hour or so to reach the riverbed at the very bottom of the Canyon. Warnings (below) along the trail advise hikers of the many hazards.

WARNING
Do Not Continue Unless You Have
WATER & FOOD
There Is No Water For 1½ Miles
Carry ½ Gallon Water
Minimum Per Person

When Mules Pass
Stand Quietly On Side Of Trail

Two million people visit the Grand Canyon annually, and the journey on muleback along the twisting Bright Angel Trail (previous pages, above, facing page bottom and overleaf) is very popular. Although the descent, along switchbacks cut into the steep cliffs, seems formidable, the reliable mules have not had an accident in over 50 years and no rider has come to harm. Safety rules dictate that all riders must be over 12 years old and under 200 pounds in weight. Left and facing page top: views from Mather Point Lookout, named after the first director of the National Park Service.

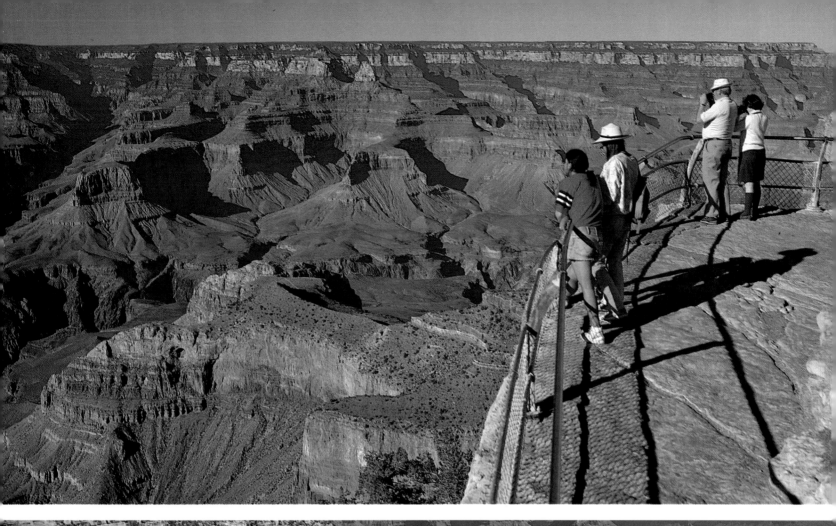

These pages: views of Bright Angel Trail. Overleaf: the Grand Canyon pictured from Mather Point Lookout, from which most visitors get their first view of the Canyon. Barely a quarter of the entire Canyon can be seen from Mather Point, as the National Park is made up of more than a million acres, embracing more than 277 miles of the Colorado River.

The Visitor Center (left) of Grand Canyon National Park houses exhibits on the natural history of the Canyon, and Rangers are on duty daily to help answer visitors' questions and plan tours of the Canyon. It is largely the swiftly-flowing Colorado River, (below and facing page, overleaf and following pages) that has created the Canyon landscape. Some 25 million years ago it began to scour the flat plateau, cutting through layer after layer of rock. The oldest rocks exposed in the Grand Canyon were formed about 2 billion years ago. Some 1,700 million years ago these were thrust up into mountains, only to be almost entirely eroded away. This process continued, slowly adding to the complex layers of rock.

Previous pages and facing page bottom: late evening light bathes the Canyon as seen from Mohave Point on the South Rim. Facing page: (top) the Canyon viewed from near Hopi Point, named after the Hopi Indians, who live 100 miles east of the Canyon. Right: late evening visitors view the Canyon from Pima Point. The point is named for the Pima Indians of south-central Arizona. Below: an aerial view over the Temple Butte area, and (overleaf) mysterious light on the Canyon landscape below West Rim Drive.

Parts of the Canyon appear extremely barren (facing page top), whereas other areas support sparse vegetation (left and facing page bottom). Below: the Palisades of the Desert seen from Desert View Lookout, and (overleaf) the Battleship, dramatically lit, viewed from Pima Point. Following pages: (left top) an information board at Studio Lookout, and (left bottom) scrub-covered slopes viewed from the El Tovar Hotel area. Right top: a panorama beyond Desert View, and (right bottom) shelving cliffs and scree slopes.

The Grand Canyon—
1,800 million years of sedimentation, erosion, and life.

Permian

Mississippian

Pennsylvanian

Devonian

Cambrian

Precambrian

Previous pages: eroded cliffs seen from Desert View Lookout, and (above and left) early morning light at Mather Point. Facing page: (top) the jade-colored Colorado River, and (bottom) Studio Lookout over Bright Angel Trail. Overleaf: the Battleship seen from Pima Point at sunset, with Wotans Throne and Vishnu Temple on the horizon. Following pages: (left top and right top) soft evening sunlight seen from Desert View Lookout. Left bottom: Yavapai Point at sunrise, and (right bottom) daybreak at Hopi Point.

Previous pages: blue ridges recede into the distance from East Rim Drive. Facing page: (top) Duck on a Rock Viewpoint, and (bottom) the Canyon seen from Grand View Point. Above: multicolored cliffs beyond Grand View Point, and (right) the National Park entrance. The Canyon's walls (overleaf) were cut not only by the Colorado River, but by rain and melting snow, and their height was increased by the upward force of subterranean pressures.

GRAND CANYON NATIONAL PARK

NATIONAL PARK SERVICE
UNITED STATES DEPARTMENT OF THE INTERIOR

NATIONAL PARK SERVICE
Department of the Interior

Previous pages: (left top) layered cliffs, (left bottom) the Kaibab Trail, (right top) the Watchtower, and (right bottom) the little Colorado River. Bottom: Havasu Falls. Facing page: (top) backpackers walking to Havasu Falls, and (bottom) sunset over the Canyon.

Havasu Canyon is located
some 40 miles northwest of
Grand Canyon Village. The
lush greenery and abundance
of water at Havasu Falls
(previous pages, facing
page bottom and overleaf)
is in refreshing contrast
to the largely arid
landscape of the Canyon.
Two miles north of the
falls lies Havasupai Indian
Village (above), where
there are two tourist
lodges from which visitors
can explore the surrounding
country. Left: brilliant
cactus flowers, and (facing
page top) Havasu Canyon
near Havasu Falls.

Previous pages: Havasupai Indian Village, (above) an Indian guide, (left) Wotans Throne and Vishnu Temple in the sun's last rays, (top left) green Havasu Canyon, and (top) backpackers near Havasu Falls. Facing page: (top) outcrop in Marble Canyon area and (bottom and overleaf) rafting expedition preparations in Marble Canyon.

Vivid wildflowers (these
pages) enliven the
desert's colors. Overleaf:
a rafting expedition on
the Colorado River at
Marble Canyon.

Exhilarating river rides are one way of experiencing the grandeur of the Marble Canyon (above, top right, facing page bottom and overleaf), where sheer cliffs rise 800 feet on each side of the Colorado. Top, right and facing page top: views of the Marble Canyon area.